# "Oo do 'ee think 'ee are?"

A short introduction to the Devonshire Dialect

Includes the stories - 'A Case of Horse-stealing', and 'What us zeed, dued, 'an yurd at Bampton Vair', as well as a local dialect dictionary.

Compiled and Edited by Jason D C Sullock

For more Devonshire genealogy, local history and events, follow Jason Sullock on Twitter at @DevonGenealogy or visit www.WestCountry-Genealogy.co.uk

## An Introduction to the Devon Dialect

The Devon accent has the westcountry 'burr' that is common to south-west Britain, and until the 19th century, the it was largely protected from outside influences, due to its geographical isolation.

In more recent times, West Country dialects have been treated with some derision, and there is a popular prejudice that Devonians, and indeed West Country speakers as a whole, are unsophisticated and even backward. This has led many local speakers to abandon their accent. This is a genuine shame, as recent studies of trustworthiness rate the West Country accent highly... below southern Scots-English, but a long way above London Cockney, or Scouse, the accent of Liverpool.

Indeed, contrary to many people's beliefs, the Devon dialect is not a debased, backward or corrupted form of modern English, but the evolved version of the original English language, descended in particular from the Late West Saxon, which spread across England from the time of King Alfred in the tenth century.

Although referring to Somerset, Lt-Col. J. A. Garton's observation in 1971, could equally apply to Devon:

"Many words, thought to be wrongly pronounced by the countryman, are actually correct, and it is the accepted pronunciation which is wrong. English pronounces W-A-R-M worm, and W-O-R-M wyrm; in the dialect W-A-R-M is pronounced as it is spelt, Anglo-Saxon W-E-A-R-M. The Anglo-Saxon for worm is W-Y-R-M. Polite English pronounces W-A-S-P wosp; the Anglo-Saxon word is W-O-P-S and a Somerset man still says WOPSE. The verb To Be is used in the old form, I be, Thee bist, He be, We be, Thee 'rt, They be. 'Had I known I wouldn't have gone', is 'If I'd a-know'd I 'ooden never a-went'

The classic phrase in the Devonshire dialect is 'her told she' and a gentleman named Cecil Torr was once told by a religious Devonian 'us didn't love He, twas Him loved we'. Another notable phrase is 'us be' or 'we am' instead of 'we are' - and this is often contracted into 'we'm'.

What is less well known is that Devon was one of the last places to speak the Celtic language in what is now England - where its speech died out in the Middle Ages - but remained in numerous place names, surnames, and a number of words retained by the Devon dialect.

For example, as any casual observer of place names will soon notice, the incidence of combe or coombe place names in Devon is extremely high, numbering in the hundreds. The word or suffix 'combe' comes from the Celtic for valley. Combe is not unique to Devon but in no other county is it as commonly used. This usage dates back to the earliest records and it appeared in 64 Devon place names in the Domesday book.

As well as a dialect dictionary, I have included two short stories in this book to illustrate how the words and grammar were and - in some cases - still are actually used. For me these not only give the reader an insight into the level of education of our ancestors, but also provide a glimpse into Devonian society – as was – as well as highlighting the often light-hearted nature of their view of the world... enjoy.

**"A Case of Horse-stealing"**

*From stories told by Sir Stafford Northcote" - 1st Lord Iddesleigh (1818 – 1887)*

A man of the name of J.B. was accused of having stolen a horse, and one of his neighbours had been summoned to attend the trial as a witness. The lawyer, after having asked him a few questions, proceeded thus in cross-examination:

Lawyer – You know J.B.

Witness – Yes, your Honner.

Lawyer – Did he ever say anything to you about the horse?

Witness – Well, I'll tell your Honner just how 'twas. The other day I said to him 'How about the horse?' and he said to me 'He didn't know nothing about the horse.'

Lawyer – Stop now witness, that's very important; tell me what he really did say?

Witness – It was just that yer Honner. I said to him 'How about the horse?' And he said to me 'He didn't know nothing about the horse'.

Lawyer – He didn't say *he* did not know anything about the horse.

Witness – Yes he did. D'ye think I'd tell yer Honner a lie?

Lawyer – You don't understand what I mean; he did not speak to you in the third person.

Witness – There weren't no third person there, there was only him and me.

Lawyer – No, no; but I mean, I suppose that he spoke to you in the first person.

Witness – No a didn't; I was the first person spoke to he, and I says to he 'How about the horse?' And he says to me 'A didn't know nothing about the horse'.

Here the judge thought it time to interfere and clear up the difficulty, and he said 'Stop. Now witness" - attend to me; this is what I suppose took place. You said to him – 'How about the horse?'

Witness – Yes yer Honner, I did.

Judge – Well, then he said to you 'I don't know anything about the horse'.

Witness – No yer Honner, he didn't; he never once mentioned yer Worship at all.

## **"What us zeed, dued, 'an yurd at Bampton Vair"**

*From 'Zummerzet Folk and Devonshire Diversions'*

1925

Although I've a lived in thease parts zo many year
I'd niver bin tu Bampton vair till thease year.

Twuz Jan Chidgey that got me to goo, vor Jan du niver miss 'et ef he can 'ulp et. He zaid tw'ud "brighten me up like," an that t'wud be "a capital opportunity o' studyin' 'uman natur'."

I nawtiss that whenever Jan du goo off to anjoy hizzel, he du always try to maaike volks belaive that he du goo more as a stoodent o' mankind than anythin' else. Jan du dearly love a chaange an'a bit of vun - but bein' a Daicon up to th' Baptisses it du behove un not tu appear tu worldly like - but still he be zo straight as a line in all his dailins, an' there's no reason why he shud'dn eendulge his soshual instinks now an' then.

Wul I zaid, I'd goo an' study 'uman natur long wi' un, an zee he ded'n get into no mischief; zo on Thursday us started off vrom Tiverton by th' airly morning' train an' got to Bampton 'bout 'alf pas' nine.

Tez a vunny lid'l plaace is Bampton; an turble old vashioned. Just wan stragglin' strait an' nothin' gwain on all the year 'cept when the 'oss and pony vair be held in Octawber - an then the plaace is sight tu zee an' no mistake.

As us wuz comin' along een the train I got taalkin' wi the jolly old urd-faaced varmers an' larned a lot 'bout 'osses an' ponies. They du bring een scores an' hundreds of li'l ponies vrom Axmoor. Zome on 'em ban't no biggeren' Noofoundlan' dugs" - but they'm brave an' smart an' when they'm prapperly brawk 'een, they be zold to draa Bath Cheers, an' gov'ness cars an' the likes o' that. Zince the bikes an' mortars come 'een, there idd'n quite the demand vor em there used to be. Still, they du zell a gude lot every year, an' it's a purty sight tu see he lid'l dears drawved een vrom the moors, an' 'undreds o' volk du come zimply vor tu enjy the vun an 'vrolie.

As soon as us arrived Jan said us must goo straight up tu th' orchet enclosure, where th' auctioneer, Muster Blackvord o' South Molton, be gwain tu conduck the saale.

Zous volleyed th' crowd dru the strait, but what wi' the shaip, an' bullocks, an 'osses, tu say nuthin' o' the volks crowdin' round the Fairin' booths, an'

Chape Jacks, et tuk us th' best part of haafe an' hour vore us got to th' plaace where th' plaace where the ponies wuz tu.

'Twuz a bit drizzly an' as vor the muck undervoot, 'twuz like wadin' droo pay-soup, but no wan ded'n zeem vor to mind. There wuz scores o' rail gen'lmen an' laaidies what had come een their mortar cars, tu zee the zight of a lifetime, an they was laughin' an' jokin' as if they wuz enjyin' o their zels prapper an' no mistake.

There wuz just time vor us to zee the ponies all crammed up together behind a lot o' hurdles, an' then all to wance a beel wuz ringed as a zignal that the zaale wuz about tu begin. Jan an' I co'ced our way dru the crowd, an' by payin' a shullin' aich us wuzadmitted tu the covered stand' where Mr Blackvord wuz vaacin' the gurt crowd o' people what wuz pressin' round the ring where the ponies wuz tu shaw off their paaces.

Everybody zeemed up vor a bit o' vun, an' as vor 'uman natur, us had it there in all its aspicks. Drovers an' Varmers, Gypsy Chaps in checks an' velvet coats wi' pearl buttons an' urd an' yaller 'andkychifs round their necks, schule bwoys an' shaffers, Landlords an' Lab'rers, there they wuz, all chack by jowl, vor as the Poet du zay "wan touch o' Natur' du make the whole worlde kin!"

Then Mr Blackvord beginned the zaale. Law, how the veller can talk! Volks zay that years agone he wuz a hactor 'pon the stage, an' I can well belaive it. A trim, well groomed, dapper zort o' man, wi' a urd vaace an' wax ends tu his mustaches, like the picturs us zees o' the German Emperor, an' a voice like a bewl. He can go on all day wi'out turnin' a 'air, I'm tould.

"Gentleman" says Mr Blackvord, "we be now arrived at wan o' th' most important events in 'uman 'istory. This be Bampton Vair! an' tis wll knawed that wance a year all the worlde an' is wive do goo to Bampton! This is the vorty-zixth year my firm has sold at this 'istoric vair, an we have here wan o' the gurtest conglomerations o' gude, bad an indifferent people that is possible to procure in the Kengdom."

Wull, when he taalked away a bit in thik vree an genial style, he rayminded them of the conditions of zaale and zet to work in gude airnest. The virst lot of ponies wuz Gaarge Taylor's up to Brendon, an' twuz vun an' no mistake to hear the bits o' chaff between Gaarge an' Mr Blackvord. Thease tu zeemed tu be old vriends an' ded'n mind a bit what they zaid wan' t'other. Mr Blackvord gied Gaarge a cigar an' told 'un to light up as tw'ud keep'n braave an' happy while the ponies wuz bein' zold.

Then wan of the ponies wuz turned 'een, an' did'n he rish round an' round the ring like a maazed thing.

"The fust hoss is a mare," said Mr Blackvord "a riglar li'l buty, now varmer Gaarge perambulate ef yu plaize – vancy you'm Lard Gaarge Sanger vor wance."

"Yu dry up," shouted Gaarge, "I be a candidate vor old-age pinshuns." The crowd began laafin but Mr Blackvord zaid: "Now then ladies and gentleman, we have a little vun, but a gurt dail o' bezness. How much vor the mare? Property of Mr Taylor o' Brendon, an' zold vor no vault whatever!"

Wul, the li'l baste were zold vor dree poun' an' law the trouble they had to get'n out o' the ring tu maake rume vor the next comer!

The plucky little beggar rished all awver the plaace, an tried to git out every cornder but the right wan. The laadies laughed till they cried tu zee his antics, an' Mr Blackvord holleyed out to Dan Fishleigh to luke sharp as he wad'n gwaine to waaste his time – "Time is money at Bampton Vair," he said.

"Now ladies, kindly modulate your vices ef you plaaize. You are not at a village Bazaar or a Jumble Zale, neither is this I sh'ud apply for a zipperation arder. An' yet they wonder why zome men take to drink!"

This quieted the ladies, an' at last Dan Fishleigh is desperation tuk the li'l pony up in he's arms, an' carried un tu the plaace he wanted'n tu goo, an' off the li'l baste galloped, like the wind, up tu the orchet enclosure, where he wuz zoon jined by others, what had bin knacked down vor various prices by the auctioneer.

Wul, us stayed on the stand a braave while, an' about twulve o'clock, us began to veel wommly in th' innards. Zo Jan an' I left Mr Blackvord tu zee the zaale dru, an' off us went up tu the 'White 'Oss' vor a bit o' denner. Uz wuz amongst the vust to go 'een an' a gude jawb, vor latter on the plaace wuz besaiged wi' vaminishin' varmers, but us had a gude steart o' they, an' vor tu shillin' us had a prapper denner an' no mistake.

At wan aind o' th' table there wuz a gurt big round o' biled baif, wi' carrots, taters, turmuts, an cabbidge; an' all the way down th' taable wuz suet puddins' zo big as cannon balls. There wuz also roast baif, an' the carvers had their work cut out I warn to kaip up wi' the demand. Of coorse there wuz plenty of zider, but Jan an' I ded'n touch the twoading old stuff, as us is both taytottlers.

Us maade it up in puddin' though, an' the 'White Oss' people ded'n get a braave lot o' profit out of we I reg'n. We ordered a jug o' water as an example tu the rest, an Jan gied the 'ooman sixpence tu shaw that taytottlers can be generous as well as virtuous.

By this time us wuz raddy to traapse round "an rape the 'arvest of a quiet heye" as Jan put it 'een his ushual poetickle style.

Us wuz turble tuk up wi' the Chape Jacks. Law! How they vellers can taalk! What lawkle praichers they'd maake ef they turned their talons tu prapper account! An how daid in airnest they be, not like zome praichers who talk like men in a draim an' dawn't ever expect to gain a verdict wan way or tother.

How they chapsworked tu be get volks tu buy their gudes! Wan wuz zellin' second-'and clothin': "Gentlemen," he zays, "this watterprufe coat wuz maade vor a British Awficer o' the 'ighest rank, but twuz a bit ew tight onder th'arms, an' zo Ican offer it chape. Look at the linin' all silk! I'll put it on backsivore zo as you can zee the stripes o' thik butival linin.'

"Now gentlemen, 'ow much vor th' watterprufe? Wance the property of a awficer een th' Life Guards. Et cost the best part o' vower pound when it left the 'ands of a 'igh class London tailor. Yu shall ha en vor vefty shillin' vor forty, vor thirty vive, vor thirty, vor twenty-sebben an' six. For a sovereign. Now look 'ere! Don't you know a bargain when yo zee it? Yu bain't a lot o' loonatics, but zensible main. Look at the coat, look at the linin', I'm givin' it away!

"Look 'ere! I'm not gwain tu zay that thik coat'll kaip out the waters o' Niaggerer which vlows in all its thundrin cataracks at the rate o' tew hundred an' vifty million tons a minit, but I do zay that if yu be out on the moors an' downs in twulve hours' rain in tempest or in starm, yu'll come 'ome wi' a dry shart!

"An' if yu stan' there gaapin' til your toe nails pinitrate dru your butes, I won't zell'n vor less than sbenteen shillin'."

Well that last burst o' oratory vetched 'em, an' a man in the crowd bought the coat an' paid vor'n, an' put'n on, ther an' then, while the auctioneer fetched out another article an' began his patter wance more.

Taalkin' of langwidge, there wuz wan chap who taalked like a prented buke. He bagan by showin' a few li'l gowlden discs like 'arf suvrins. He plaaced wan o' these 'pon zome li'l cardboard boxes, but this was only to draa the attention. When he'd got his audience he zays "Now yu zee I've got a golden token 'pon aich of these boxes, an' the objick I have in vu is tu interest yu in what is een these boxes." He then took out a curious lookin' objick an' commenced to spaik about et.

" I have 'ere a small mechanikkle hinstrooment, wan o' the greatest wonders hof the age. Accordin' to the way yu holds this 'highly scientific hinstrooment, it becomes a Raidin' Glass, a Microscope, a Tiliscope, a Hopera Glass, a Steery-o-skop *or* a Compass.

"I raise this arm an' you have a raidin' glass to assist the failin' sight o' lite'ry stoodents, I raise another perpendic'lar arm, an' by means o' the two horizontal crystals I now have a mikryscope of amazin' magnifyin' power. Notice these zeeds 'pon the back o' my and. Millet-zeeds they may be, but look at 'em dru the mikryscope, an they'm as big as cherry stones. By means of this hinstrument yu can deteck mikrobes in a glaws o' water, an vleas 'll luke like black-baidles. Any gen'lman can test this vor hisself vor vleas is plentivul in thease parts likewise mikrobes. No intellekshual person should be without this remarkable scientific hinstrooment.

“Now nawtiss that by raisin’ wan large and wan small lens, you get a Pocket Tiliscope, zo that when yu du go to the Zay Zide vor the day, yu can scan the ‘orizon an’ make out the naame an ‘nashunality of any vessel in the hoffing. Yu can slide this part dru an’ vro to suit all Zights. Then again if yu be at the Hoppera or any other plaace o’ public hentertainment, by elevatin’ vower o’ these lenses yu get a hopper glaws of a most powerful charriter.

“An’ when ‘tis tu wet to go out o’doors, by reversin’ the hinstrooment yu gets what is called a steeryo-skop, by means of which yu can spend a ‘appy winter evenin’ at ‘ome, lookin’ at picture postcards and pottygrafts. Then wance more by raisin' this one bar, and inclin' this part to a angle of vorty vive degrees, you attain what is prob'ly one of the most vallyable medical hinstrooments in existence. You have now what Doctor call a larryingeo-skop, by means o' which yu can deteck ulsters in the droat, polypusses in the nawse, an' which du magnify the surface of the eye to that extent that disaises in the himportant horgin can be located with the greatest ease.

"An larstly by 'oldin' the hinstrooment vlat upon your 'and, or puttin' it on any stationary objick such as a taable or pianner, yu get a compass which 'll guide 'e home in the darkest nights.

"Gentlemen do I ex-agg-erate when I claim that I 'old in my 'and one of the greatest scientific triumphs o' this most progressive age?

"An' what is the price, you harsk? Well, in Americ, these hinstrooments is never sold onder two dollars, which is a little over eight shillin' o' English money. I only have seven left of these interestin' instructive, an' hedicatin' scientific hinstrooments! My price is within the reach of the humblest mechanic or labourer. It's only two shillin'! It's the chance of a lifetime!"

By this time the crowd was purty near heep-no-tized, an several of the things was bought. Jan wanted to buy wan to car' 'ome, but he resisted the temptation, vor he knawed that Mrs Chidgey 'd gie un a purty old taalkin' to ef he drawed away his money on fantastical Chape Jack Trade. Still 'twuz a wonderful thing ef tw'ud railly du all the man claimed vor't. The man zeemed straight enough an' gave away a paaper o'draxions and an' diagrams to aich purchaser zo that he'd knaw azactly 'ow to work the deffer'nt lenses when he got hawm.

Wul us traipsed all dru' th' vair together. There wuz wan man standin' up 'pon a carriage, pretendin' to zell sovrins vor shellins. Several gawkums wuz tuk 'een wi' his patter an' cheap joolry an' watches, but arter a bit the crowd began to hustle th' old rascal, an he was hooted all the way to th' stashun, an' ef it had'n bin vor the police they'd a sar-d un' a bad an' he'd a deserved it too, the schemin' old twoad.

Jan 'n I went in to wan Public 'ouse where there wuz a lot o' gipsies an' low class labrers enjoyin' o' theirzels but a vew minits there wuz enough for us. The same rume was packed wi' volks in deffernt staages o' exuberation. Several gals wuz in there tew, braazen faaced uzzies, wi' veathers in their 'ats as bowld as Lions. 'Twuz a zad zight to think that this wuz the 'ighest 'appiness such volk desired. There wuz a bwoy playin' a mouth orgin zo ard's he cud goo – zaame toon all the time – an' every now an' then a gipsy chap 'ud taake th' vloor" - shut 'is eyes, an begin' to dance, an' he wud kip on as long as lags an' lungs 'd last. Then he wud retire amid clappin' o' 'ands, taake a drink o' zider, while another wud begin tu daance.

Poor Blids! My 'art velt zad as I went out o' thik public 'ouse. I velt more'n ever I ded what blessin' 'twuz to be a tay-tottler. But thank God, things iddn nearly zo bad's they used to be. There wad'n a treble lot o' drunk'ness tu Bampton, an' as vur as I cud zee the volks, though vroliszome, wuz paicable an' well conducted.

"Tez just zo wul," as Jan Chidgey zays, "to get out o' your ordinary gruve now an' again, an' zee what's g'wain on."

I be glad I went awver tu Bampton, but tid'n very likely I shall goo agin, vor tez zackly the zame zort o' thing every year, an' when yuve gone the round, yuve had enough vor a lifetime. Bezides I cud'n goo again vor missis wud'n let me tu, an' that's the truth ef yu must knaw the rail raison why I do eentend to stap hawm een the future!

## A Devonshire Dialect Dictionary

Aa

"A Lady Dishwasher" – Bird, Pied Wagtail. Describing The Way It's Tail Goes Up And Down Like A Dishwasher's Tongue Gossiping.

"A Proper Country Janny" - Someone Who Is Old Fashioned Or Puritanical.

"Ab-Dab" - To Bluff Someone.

"Abs" Or "Asp" - An Abscess.

"Acker" - Acre.

"Affeard" - Afraid.

"Ageest" - Afraid/Astonished.

"Agging" - Egging On, Raising Quarrels.

"Ago" - Just Gone, as in Nearly Dead.

"Agoon" - Soon.

"Akether" - Quoth He.

"Alaska" - I'll Ask Her.

"Alkitotle" - A Silly Elf.

"All Abroad" - Open, As In "The Door Is All Abroad".

"Allernbatch" - An Old Sore.

"Ammulling" - Covered In Moisture.

"An" – Than, As In "More An Zo", More Than So.

"Aneest" - Near, As In "I Wont Go Aneest En".

"Angings" - Door Hinges.

"Ansney" - To Anticipate Bad News.

"Appen" - Perhaps.

"Aprill'd" - Soured, Or Turning Sour.

"Apurt" - Sullen Or Silent With A Gloating.

"Aquott" - Squatted, Or Weary Of Eating.

"Arable" - Horrible.

"Arg" - To Argue Or Dispute.

"Art" - Eight.

"Arteen" - Eighteen.

"Aslat" - Cracked Like A Pot.

"Asneger" - An Ass.

"Auvis" - The Eaves Of A Building.

"Avroar" - Frozen Or Frosty.

"Awpway" - An Alleyway.

Bb

"Baa Samb Saish" - A Sheep Gate.

"Bacon Ore" - The Mineral Barytes Found In Layers.

"Bagging Out" - Workmen Taking Packed Lunches To Work.

"Bak" - To Beat.

"Bal" - To Strike Someone.

"Ballyrag" - To Scold.

"Barra" - A Gelt Pig.

"Barton" - Historically The Farm Of The Local Squire.

"Bate" - To Quarrel.

"Bed Ale" - Ale Brewed For A Christening.

"Bee Lippen" - A Bee Hive.

"Being/Bin" - Because.

"Bellyharm" - The Colic.

"Belve" - The 'Moo' Of A Cow.

"Bescummer" - To Foul With Dirty Linen.

"Bettermass" - Better Than Usual.

"Bettermost Folk" - The Gentry Or Upper Classes.

"Betwit" - To Upbraid/Repeat A Matter.

"Bezooks" - To Go Berserk.

"Bibble" - To Drink Often.

"Billid" - Distracted/Mad.

"Bittle" - A Mallet.

"Biver" - To Shake/Quiver.

"Black Army" - Fleas.

"Black Thrush" - A Blackbird.

"Blid" - Blood.

"Bloggy" - To Be Sullen.

"Boostering" - To Labour Busily So As To Sweat.

"Bote" - Past Tense Of To Buy.

"Bowerly" - Blooming, As In "A Comely Bowerly Woman".

"Brack" - A Flaw

"Braith" - Hedge Trimmings.

"Braithe" - To Repair Fences.

"Britchin" - Harness For A Horse.

"Buckle" - A Struggle.

"Buddled" - Suffocated.

"Bulhaggle" - A Scarecrow.

"Bus Cav" - A Suckling Calf.

"Buster" - Something Obstinate And Difficult To Overcome.

Cc

"Caal/Caaling" - A Call.

"Calathumpian" - A Chapel-Goer.

"Canvas" - An Oilcloth Or Linoleum Floor. I Suspect – but have no proof - This Came From The Habit Of Painting A Black And White Checker On A Sailing Canvas And Laying It In A Captain's Cabin On Board A Ship, To Give The Illusion Of A Stone Floor.

"Carbender"" - "Gramper-Griggs"" - And "Gramper-Sow" - A Wood-Louse.

"Carrot" - Simile" - As In "As Smart As A Carrot". To Look Good.

"Cats" - Pies.

"Cawbaby" - An Awkward Timid Bod.

"Cham" - I Am.

"Change Of Days" - The Solstice.

"Chattermag" - A Gossip.

"Chave" - I Have.

"Chell" - I Shall.

"Chets" - Kittens.

"Chilbladder" - Chilblains.

"Chinking Grass" - The New Growth Of Grass In Early Spring.

"Chinny Reckon" - A Tall Tall" - Especially From A Fisherman.

"Choogie-Pig" - The Runt Of A Litter.

"Chrisemore" - An Unchristened Child.

"Chups" - Cheeks/Chops.

"Churn" - A Bad Woman.

"Claggy" - Sticky.

"Clathers" - Clothes.

"Clear And Sheer" - Completely/Totally.

"Cleves" - Cliffs.

"Cloof" - Well Fed. Usually Referring To Cattle.

"Clopping" – Lame, Limping.

"Clume Buzza" - An Earthenware Pan.

"Coalvarty" - A Bed Or To Warm A Bed With A Warming Pan.

"Cob/Clobb" – Mud, Loam And Straw Building.

"Cockabel" - An Icicle.

"Cockhedge" - A Quick Built Hedge

"Cockleert" - When Cock Crows.

"Cole" - Any Kind Of Cabbage.

"Combe" - A Hollow Between Two Hills Open At One End Only.

"Commercing" - As in talking or Conversing.

"Condiddle" - To Waste Or Convey Away Secretly.

"Condudle" - Conceit.

"Conflooption" - A Fuss.

"Coot" - The Iron Round Heel Of A Boot.

"Copper Finch" - A Chaffinch.

"Corbett" - A Wooden Tub For Salting A Pig.

"Corniwillin" - A Lapwing.

"Corrosy" - A Grudge Or Ill-Will.

"Cort" - Caught.

"Cotten" - To Beat Soundly.

"Couch Pawed/Handed" - Awkward/Left-Handed.

"Courtlage" - The Fore Or Backyard Of A House.

"Cow And Calf" - Cider And Guiness.

"Cow Comfort" - A Scratching Post.

"Cowal" - A Fish-Woman's Basket.

"Cozing/Coozing" - Loitering/Soaking.
"Crab's Eye Boil" - Not Quite Boiling.

"Crazed" - Cracked" - As In Insane

"Crewdling" - Sensible Of Cold.

"Crewnting" - Grunting/Complaining.

"Crickle" – To Bend.

"Cricks" - Dry Hedgewood.

"Crimps" - Adjective" - To Be Brittle.

"Crocky Stew" - Potato Stew.

"Cropeing" - Stingy.

"Crowst" - Elevenses.

"Cruel" - Very" - As In "It Weren't Cruel Fair".

"Crummit" - A Snack Eaten Between Meals.

"Cuttin" - To Be Precise In The Usage Of Words.

Dd

“Dab Washin'“ - Rinsing Clothing.

“Dab” - To Be Good At Something” - As In “Eee Were A Dab 'And”.

“Daggle” - To Run Like A Young Child.

“Dally-Law” - A Spoilt Child.

“Daps” - The Exact Likeness Of.

“Daver” - To Fade Like A Flower.

“Dawcock” - A Silly Fellow.

“Deef” - Rotten/Corrupted.

“Deeve's Paust” - As Deaf As A Post.

“Desperd” - Very/Extremely.

"Diddlecome" - Half-Mad/Sorely Vexed.

"Didikai" - A Gypsy.

"Dimmet" - The Dusk Of The Evening.

"Dimpty" - Twilight.

"Dinder" - Thunder.

"Dirsh" - A Thrush.

"Dish" - Method Of Spoking A Wheel, As In "We Spoke The 'Dish' Of The Wheel".

"Dishwater" - Water Wagtail.

"Dittyguys" - Corruption Of Didichai Or Gypsies.

"Dizzen" - A Dozen.

"Do" - To Be Done, As In "To Be Do".

"Doan" – Wet, or Damp Bread.

"Doattie" - To Nod The Head In Sleep While Sitting Up.

"Doattie" - Nodding

"Doll" - To Toll, Like A Bell.

"Dollop" - A Portion.

"Don/Doff" - To Put On/Off.

"Donykin" - The Privy Or Earth Closet At The Bottom Of The Garden.

"Doughy" - Mentally Slow.

"Dowsty Poll" - A Dusty Head, From Flour Or Dust.

"Dozey-Frizzle" - An Old Woman, Or A Man Who Is Acting Like An Old Woman.

"Drayed" - To Have Your Picture Drawn Or Photograph Taken.

"Drescoll" - The Threshold Of A Building.

"Dresher" - A Dresser.

"Drixy" - Dry Or Brittle.

"Drot" - Throat.

"Droysh" - To Thrash Someone.

"Droysher" - A Boot.

"Dudder" - To Deafen With Noise.

"Dumbledore" - A Bee.

"Dummon" - An Old Woman.

Ee

"Eart" - Sometimes.

"Eats Like A Hedger" - To Have A Good Appetite.

"Ee Gone Over Cross" - Said Of Someone Who Has Gone Into Cornwall Over The Tamar River".

"Ee' Gone Cross" - Said Of A Soldier Who Has Been Posted Abroad.

"Eedy-Peep" - To Spy From Cover.

"Ellem Tree" - Elm Tree.

"Elong" - Slanting.

"Elsh" - New.

"En" – Him, As In "I Told En".

“Er've Got A Good Tail” - A Widow Who Has Several Children Handicapping Her Chances Of Another Marriage.

“Es,Ise,Ish” - I.

“Eth” - Earth.

“Eute” - Pour Out.

“Evel” - A Four Pronged Dung Fork.

“Every Whip N Trip” - Now And Again.

Ff

"Fadge" - To Fare As In "How D'ye Fadge?"

"Farmer's Friend" - Binder Twine.

"Farmer's Livery" - Jute Sacks, Often Worn To Protect A Farmer In Bad Weather.

"Feeling Fairy" - In Good Health.

"Fig-Airy" - Much Ado About Nothing.

"Fitty" - Clever.

"Flare" - The Layer Of Fat Under Streaky Bacon.

"Flickets" - Flushes In The Face.

"Fore-Right" - An Honest Person.

"Fuddicking" - To Prod Or Poke Something.

“Fump” - Essence Of.

## Gg

"Gammicking" - Playing Games.

"Ganmer" - Mistress/An Old Woman.

"Gatfer" - An Old Man.

"Gawk" - Stupid.

"Go Quott" - To Go Quiet Or Lie Low.

"Gommel" - An Idiot.

"Gone On" - To Have Died.

"Goob" - A Silly Person.

"Good Openin' Weather" - The First Hard Frost Of The Year.

"Grainy" - Superior.

"Grammer" - Grandmother

"Granfer" - Grandfather

"Grockle Shell" - A Caravan.

"Grockle" - A Derogatory Term For A Tourist.

"Grutti" - The Devil.

"Guddle" - To Drink Greedily.

"Gude - Bedder - Bedderer - More Bedderer – Beddermos' - Bes - Bestest" – Good To Best.

"Guit" - A Joint.

"Gurt Dough-Bake" - A Simpleton.

"Gurt" - Big.

"Gykes" - Habits.

Hh

"Hairy Farmers" - Woolly Bear Caterpillars.

"Harried" - To Gossip About, Or Be Gossiped About.

"Hatch" - Fancy Wish.

"He May Move Mortstone" - Said In Response To Someone Who Is Boasting.

"Hell" - To Pour.

"Hen Avore Day" - To Take Too Long Or Prevaricate, As In "Like A Hen Avore Day".

"Hend" - To Throw.

"Heppitude" - To Hop To It, Or Get On With It.

"Hickety Hackety" - Untidy.

"Hoop" - A Bullfinch.

"Horsepacks" - Old Pack-Horse Roads.

"Hulder" - To Hide Or Conceal

"Hulve" - To Turn Over

## Ii

"Idden Zackly" - Not Well. From "He/She Isn't Exactly All There".

"In Country" - To Be Off Dartmoor.

"It Were World Wide In This Locality" - Common Knowledge.

## Jj

"Janner" - Anyone Who Earns Their Living From The Sea.

"Jasper" - A Wasp.

"Jew" - A Flying Beetle.

"Johnny-Noddy" - The Reflection Of Light From Water Or A Piece Of Glass Or Mirror.

"Journey" - A Days Work.

"Just Light High Jail" - A Noisy Disturbance.

## Kk

"Key Of The Market" - To Be Drunk, As In "To Come Home With The Key Of The Market".

"Kiggling" - Unsafe.

## Ll

"Landwaters Out" - A Flood.

"Larancy Weather" - Tiring Weather.

"Lerrup" - A Clumsy Person.

"Lerrupers" - Big Things, As In "Those Trees Are Gurt Big Lerrupers".

"Lew" - Sheltered/Defended From Storms.

"Lidden" - A Tale/Theme/Subject.

"Lie A Bier" - Lie Dead.

"Like A Cat In A Tripe Shop" - Said Of Someone Who Is Restless.

"Linney" - A Shed.

"Longful" - Long In Regard To Time.

"Longrue" - A Long Handled Brush.

"Lop Lolly" - Someone Who Is At Another's Beck And Call.

"Louse" - A Blood Blister Caused By A Pinch.

"Loweried" - A Sulphur Looking Sky.

Mm

"Mang" - To Mix.

"Mappers" - Boys Who Talk Too Much.

"Mapsing" - Smacking Your Lips.

"Martyrous" - A Terrible Pain.

"Mazed" - Stupid Or Silly.

"Mease" - A Measure Of 600 Fish.

"Meech" - To Play Truant

"Mommet" - A Naughty Child.

"Mooter" - To Sprout.

"Mouling" - Rolling Pastry.

## Nn

"Niddick" - The Head, As In "Dun't Bide There Scratchin' Yure Niddick".

"Nitalls" - Hazel Trees.

"Nort" - Nothing.

"Nummit" - A Lunch, Especially When Eaten By A Labourer In The Field.

Oo

"Old Man Crook" - A Goblin.

"Ordained" – Decided, As In "I Ordained To Go".

"Ort" - Anything.

"Out Ov Me Byes" - Out Of Sorts.

"Over Thickly" - Over There.

"Owlers" - Male Crabs.

## Pp

"Pakey" - Not Feeling Well.

"Pingwell" - A Blackhead.

"Pinzell" - A Boil.

"Plishing" - To Hit Hard. Also, To Lay A Hedge.

"Prake" - To Wander About.

"Praper Lil Wildergo" - An Unruly Child.

"Prapper Striver" - A Hard Worker.

"Proddling" - Milk That Has Just Risen To The Boil.

"Puddle-Hole" - A Water Outlet Or Sink.

"Pully-Alley" - Sinews Of Beef Given To Babies To Suck Dry.

"Pumble Toed" - Pigeon Toed.

## Qq

"Quarrenders" - Red Apples.

"Quasher" - The Heavy Iron Ball Used For Breaking Stone In A Quarry.

"Quilt" - To Hit Hard.

"Quithering" - A Feeling Of Apprehension Or Butterflies In The Stomach.

"Quoitch" - Sticky.

## Rr

"Raggety-Dock" - Ragged Robin.

"Ray" - To Dress.

"Readship" - Confidence, Or Trust.

"Rew Up" - To Rake Something.

"Ricksplat" - An Enclosure With Corn Ricks.

"Rislet" - A Lazy Person.

"Roady" - A Tramp.

"Roll Over To Toley" - To Roll Over In Bed.

"Rory-Dory" - Rambling.

"Rumplin Liddle Toad" - A Boasting Person.

Ss

"Said" - To Be Told, As In "Ee Wun't Be Said".

"Sally Hatch" - An Over-Dressed Woman.

"Scambling About" - To Be Untidy.

"Scannelled" - Smashed.

"Scat" - A Shower.

"Scat" - A Smack, As In To Give Someone A Smack.

"Sclum" - The Way A Cat Rakes The Furniture.

"Sclum" Or "Dree-Toed Teddy-Digger" - A Three Pronged Fork.

"Scradgerly" - Untidy.

"Scrivvens" - The Strainings Of Skin And Gristle From Fat That Has Been Rendered Down.

"Scrumps" - Apples.

"Scullen" - Wandering.

"See Yer Whenbye" - See You Tonight.

"Shab Off" - To Slink Away.

"Sheeten The Bed" - To Make-Up A Bed With Fresh Linen.

"Sherbit" - Alcoholic Drink.

"Shoog" - To Look Guilty Or Embarrassed.

"Shoot" - A Doorway Leading To A Yard.

"Shord" - A Gap In The Hedge.

"Shrammed" - To Be Cold, As In "I'm Praper Shrammed".

"Shrumpy" - Shrivelled.

"Skinter" - Skeleton.

"Skirting" Or "Velling" - Shallow Ploughing.

"Skirvetting" - Dashing Around All Over The Place.

"Skither" - Sprinkle.

"Skittle" - A Small Stain.

"Sklower" - To Scratch Yourself.

"Sladdicks" - A Two Bladed Mattock.

"Slint" - To Be Out-Of-Line, From Aslant.

"Smurry" - A Chemise.

"Snap-Dock" - Snapdragon.

"Sneath" Or "Snead" - The Handle Of A Scythe.

"Sneck" - Door Lock.

"Sno" - Do You Know.

"So Weak's A Robin" - As Weak As A Robin.

"Some Fine Friday" - Tomorrow Never Comes.

"Souti Bake" - A Simpleton.

"Spence" - A Larder Or Pantry.

"Spewmat" - Water Gushing Up Between Cobbles In A Lane From A Broken Pipe.

"Sprack" - To Be Quick.

"Spray-Wood" - Tiny Sticks Used For Lighting Fires.

"Spuddler" - Someone Who Stirs Up Trouble.

"Spurtie" - Fresh.

"Stay-Up" - To Go Out For The Evening.

"Stivver Up" - To Shake Up.

"Store Up" - To Shake Up.

"Stream" - To Rinse.

"Stugg'd" - To Be Stuck In Mud.

"Sturridges About" - To Rush About.

"Suent" – Even or Smooth.

"Suent" - To Do Something Properly, As In "Tis All Suent".

"Sull" - A Plough.

"Swant" - Proper.

"Swarte" - To Look Sullen.

"Swinkle" - To Rinse Or Ring Out.

Tt

"Taffety" - Delicate On The Palate.

"Taffity" - A Fussy Eater.

"Tang" - To Tie Something

"Teddy-Huddy" - The Devonshire Equivalent Of A Cornish Pasty But Without The Onions.

"Terrifying" - Naughty.

"Thic, Thac, They" - This That And The Other.

"Thunder And Lightning" - Treacle And Cream.

"Ticher" - A Short Distance, As In "As Near As A Ticher".

"Tiddityhops" - Fleas.

"Tilby" - Testy.

"Tilled" - To Be Ready.

"Tine" - To Shut/Close

"Titsy-Totsy" - To Be Fussy.

"Titty Todger" - A Wren.

"To Run Word" - To Break Your Word.

"To Wind And Wear It" - To Put Up With Loneliness, Especially In An Old Person.

"Tommy Taylor" - Crane Fly.

"Tormentor" Or "Skuffle" - A Cultivator.

"Totalish" - Someone Who Gone Senile.

"Trade" - To Pay For Sex, ie: Prostitution.

"Traper" - A Slut.

"Trone" - A Trench.

"Tump" - A Hill.

"Tupp" - Stupid.

"Tuppentail" - To Be Head Over Heels, To Be Happy.

"Tut-Work" - Piece-Work.

"Twily" - Troublesome Or Irksome.

## Uu

"Uffley" - A Blustering Wind.

"Under Landkey Bridge" - Go Mind Your Own Business, When Asked Where One Is Going.

"Under Th' Edge" - Something Useless. Literally Something Pushed Under The Hedge.

"Unket" – Dreary or Dismal.

"Unray" - To Undress.

"Unteel" - To Fire, As In 'To Fire A Gun'.

"Up Before The Bottomless Bodies" - Up Before The Judges. Presumably Because You Couldn't See The Judges Legs Behind The Benches.

"Up Over" - Over Dartmoor Way.

"Upsetting" - Christening

## Vv

"Vang" - To Receive/Earn.

"Vaught" - To Fetch

"Viddy" - Tidy.

"Vitty" - Sprightly.

"Vlex" - Rabbit Fur.

"Vlother" – Confused, Muddled.

"Vlower Knot" - A Flower Pot.

"Voyer-Carry" - A Barrow With Handles At Both Ends, For Carrying Earth Up A Steep Field.

"Vramin' Up A Face" - Putting On An Act.

Ww

"Want" - A Mole

"Wapping Cobwebs" - Cleaning Up.

"Ward" - To Wade.

"Washdish" - A Wagtail.

"Water-Sweet" - Said Of Something That Is Good.

"Whenbye" - Maybe.

"Whickpot" - Nonsense.

"Whims And Whams" - The Aggravating Ways Of A Person.

"Whipple Tree" - The Draft Bar For A Single Horse.

"Whiz" - To Rush About.

"Whop" - A Heavy Blow

"Widgets" - Gadgets. The Current Word Is Said To Have Been Taken To America By Devonians, Before Going World-Wide.

"Winnick" - A Weakling.

"Wisslet" - A Fool, To Be Witless.

"Wollage" - A Big Portion. Can Also Be Used To Mean An Untidy Bundle.

"Woodquist" - Wood-Pigeon

"Worrit" - Someone Who Worries, Or To Worry.

## Yy

"Y'ur's Same's That" - I Agree With You.

"Yar-Yar" - A Country-Bumpkin.

"Yearning Time" - Lambing Season.

"Yer" - The Ear, But Used In The Context Of "Yer, Listen To Me".

"Yew Mat" - A Wild Rose.

"Yewel" Or "Jewel" - A Dung Fork.

"Yous'n" - A Manager.

## Zz

"Zaitern" - A Salter.

"Zamzoe" - A Doughy Cake.

"Zat" - Soft.

"Zaundy" - To Swoon

"Zit" - Sit.

"Zo" - So

"Zoot Rad" - The Iron Bar That Goes Across A Chimney To Hang Crooks On.

"Zou Pig" - A Wood-Louse.

"Zour" - Sour.

"Zoura" - Vinegar.

"Zweemy" - To Be Dizzy.

## Further Reading

Teach yourself the Devon Dialect – BBC Link

http://www.bbc.co.uk/devon/voices2005/features/devon_dialect.shtml

## Other books by the author (available on Amazon)

'Militia of South Devon'

'Bigbury, Bigbury-on-Sea & Burgh Island, 1066-1942AD'

**About the Author**

Jason D C Sullock has been a member of the Devon Family History Society for over twenty years and began researching his genealogy in his teens.

He is the editor of several genealogy books, and regularly contributes to family history conversations through his Twitter feed @DevonGenealogy.

Jason will launch a new website www.WestCountry-Genealogy.co.uk in January 2013, with the aim of providing a portal of West Country links to fellow genealogy and local history researchers. All contributed links for inclusion on this website will be gladly accepted. If you do wish to contribute please contact Jason on Jason.sullock@westcountry-genealogy.co.uk

Jason Sullock, Teesside, UK 2012

www.ingramcontent.com/pod-product-compliance
Ingram Content Group UK Ltd.
Pitfield, Milton Keynes, MK11 3LW, UK
UKHW020219250726
13967UKWH00001B/78

9 781291 148411